First published in the United States in 1999 by Peter Bedrick Books
A division of NTC/Contemporary Publishing Group, Inc
4255 West Touhy Avenue
Lincolnwood (Chicago), Illinois 60646-1975 U.S.A.

Editor: Lisa Edwards
Designer: Kate Buxton
Language consultant: Ann Lazim,
Centre for Language in Primary Education
Natural History consultant: Michael S. Dilger

Library of Congress Cataloging-in-Publication Data
Baker, Alan.
    The rain forest / Alan Baker. − 1st American ed.
        p.   cm. −   (Look who lives in--)
    Summary: A simple introduction to the variety of animals living in
the rain forest, including butterflies, tree frogs, and iguanas.
    ISBN 0-87226-538-2 (hardcover)
    1.   Rain forest animals--Juvenile literature.   [1. Rain forest animals.]
I. Title. II Title: Look who lives in the rain forest. III. Series:
Baker, Alan, 1951-   Look who lives in--
QL 112.B35   1999
591.734--DC21   98-37562
                                                                              CIP
                                                                              AC

Printed and bound in Portugal by Edições ASA

International Standard Book Number: 0-87226-538-2

99   00   01   02   03   15   14   13   12   11   10   9   8   7   6   5   4   3   2   1

LOOK WHO LIVES IN...

The Rain Forest

ALAN BAKER

PETER BEDRICK BOOKS

NEW YORK

Deep in the dark, dank rain forest, something is looking at a spider.

It's a flitting, flapping. . .

butterfly!
It has beautiful blue and
yellow wings.
Clinging to a tiny stem, something
is looking at the butterfly.
It's a gleaming, glistening. . .

tree frog!
It has large, bright, yellow eyes.
Leaning on a curling creeper,
something is looking at the tree frog.
It's a spiny, scaly. . .

iguana!
It's got long toes and a spiny back.
Resting on a broken branch,
something is looking at the iguana.
It's a peeking, pecking. . .

13

toucan!
It's got an enormous black and orange bill.
Staring from the tall trees, something is looking at the toucan.
It's a screeching, squawking. . .

parrot!
It has brightly colored feathers and
black, beady eyes.
Resting on a sturdy log, something
is looking at the parrot.
It's a swinging, springing. . .

spider monkey!
It's got very long, gangly arms
and legs.
Hanging high up in the forest,
something is looking at the
spider monkey.
It's a squirming, worming. . .

19

boa snake!
It has a silky-smooth body and
a quick, darting tongue. Crawling
quietly along a branch, something
is looking at the boa snake.
It's a sleepy, creepy. . .

sloth!
It has long curved claws to help
it hang upside-down.
From deep within the steaming forest,
something is looking at the sloth.
It's a panting, powerful. . .

jaguar!
It has lots of black spots on his fur.
From the safety of a tree, something
is looking at the jaguar.
It's a sniffing, sucking. . .

anteater!
The anteater can see all the animals –
the jaguar, the sloth, the boa snake,
the spider monkey, the parrot, the
toucan, the iguana, the
tree frog, the butterfly
and the spider.
Can *you* see them?

The World's Rain Forests

The map below shows areas of tropical rain forest around the world. In these places it is always hot and wet. Each rain forest has different layers where different plants and animals live. Animals that can climb, swing and glide among the trees live in the top layer which is called the canopy. The canopy is made up of the branches of the tallest trees and it is the sunniest part of the rain forest.

Arctic Ocean

NORTH
AMERICA

EUROPE

ASIA

Atlantic Ocean

AFRICA

Pacific Ocean

Indian Ocean

SOUTH
AMERICA

AUSTRALIA

Southern Ocean

PAGE 7: Large spiders are some of the most common rain forest animals. They like to live on or near the damp floors of rain forests all over the world.

PAGE 8: Butterflies lay their eggs on the leaves of plants. The eggs grow into caterpillars. The caterpillars then form pupae from which fully grown butterflies hatch.

PAGE 10: Tree frogs can be green, red, orange, yellow, brown or like this one, blue. When they jump, they can glide through the air for up to 22 feet.

PAGE 13: Iguanas spend most of their time in trees, usually alongside a river or stream. They are excellent swimmers and can remain underwater for a long time.

PAGE 15: Toucans build their nests in holes inside trees, high up in the canopy. They use their bills to snip fruit from trees, and also eat insects, lizards and eggs.

PAGE 16: Parrots are very noisy and often feed in large groups. They use their beaks to help them climb and sometimes hang upside-down to reach food.

PAGE 19: Spider monkeys have long arms, legs and tails. Their tails grip on to the branches of trees. Spider monkeys are the fastest monkeys in the rain forest.

PAGE 20: Boa snakes coil themselves around the branches of trees. To kill their prey, they bite and then strangle their victim with their muscular bodies.

PAGE 22: Sloths spend most of their time hanging upside-down from tree branches. They are very slow and lazy and can sleep for up to eighteen hours each day.

PAGE 24: Jaguars are fast and agile. They are very good swimmers and like to live close to lakes and rivers. Here, they catch wild pigs, tapirs, turtles and even fish.

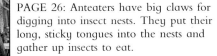

PAGE 26: Anteaters have big claws for digging into insect nests. They put their long, sticky tongues into the nests and gather up insects to eat.

Underneath the tall trees of the canopy there is very little light. This layer is called the understorey. Smaller bushes and trees grow here. Ferns, herbs and fungi grow on the dark forest floor. They grow among soil and dead leaves that have fallen from the trees above.